# HARNESSING DIGITIZATION FOR REMITTANCES IN ASIA AND THE PACIFIC

JULY 2021

ASIAN DEVELOPMENT BANK

ADB

© 2021 Asian Development Bank
6 ADB Avenue, Mandaluyong City, 1550 Metro Manila, Philippines
Tel +63 2 8632 4444; Fax +63 2 8636 2444
www.adb.org

Some rights reserved. Published in 2021.

ISBN 978-92-9262-962-5 (print); 978-92-9262-963-2 (electronic); 978-92-9262-964-9 (ebook)
Publication Stock No. TCS210263-2
DOI: http://dx.doi.org/10.22617/TCS210263-2

The views expressed in this publication are those of the authors and do not necessarily reflect the views and policies of the Asian Development Bank (ADB) or its Board of Governors or the governments they represent.

ADB does not guarantee the accuracy of the data included in this publication and accepts no responsibility for any consequence of their use. The mention of specific companies or products of manufacturers does not imply that they are endorsed or recommended by ADB in preference to others of a similar nature that are not mentioned.

By making any designation of or reference to a particular territory or geographic area, or by using the term "country" in this document, ADB does not intend to make any judgments as to the legal or other status of any territory or area.

Corrigenda to ADB publications may be found at http://www.adb.org/publications/corrigenda.

Note:
In this publication, "$" refers to United States dollars.

Cover design by Francis Manio.

# Contents

# Tables, Figures, and Boxes

# Foreword

Remittances are often referred to as the lifeline of developing countries. Their dependence on these inflows of funds from overseas workers as a source of external financing has increased steadily in the past 2 decades. Indeed, remittances into low- and middle-income countries grew from $75 billion in 2000 to $548 billion in 2019, says the World Bank. This is greater than overseas development assistance of around $166 billion and foreign direct investment of $534 billion (World Bank 2020c).

Remittances play a vital and enormous role in the lives of migrants and their families. Around 200 million migrant workers worldwide work in 40 countries and transfer money to their families of about 800 million people in more than 125 countries (International Fund for Agricultural Development 2021). The money received in migrant households in migrants' countries of origin represents about 60% of household income, which is typically spent on essential items such as food, medicines, education, and/or housing expenses. Half of this remitted money is received in rural areas, where many are poor and financially excluded (United Nations 2019b). Undeniably, cross-border remittances bring many economic benefits, boost national development, and widen financial inclusion.

Digitization has become crucial in sending and receiving countries in providing more convenience, speed, security, and affordable remittance prices. As this publication discusses, this will not only help formalize informal remittances, but can also help extend the delivery of other financial services to people scattered in remote and rural areas and areas hard to reach. While not the panacea for all issues, technology will be able to alleviate the "pain-points" in the remittances industry. Through digital data created by technology, stakeholders will gain insight. This can boost transparency and, thus, help alleviate de-risking issues and gain better understanding of consumer behavior and need. Ultimately, digitization can significantly improve the remittance experience.

The Asian Development Bank (ADB) recognizes the importance of remittances and the momentum of its support for the industry. In 2018, ADB conducted the Study on Migration and Remittances for Development in Asia (ADB 2018b). And as the coronavirus disease (COVID-19) pandemic peaked in 2020, ADB joined the Call to Action (Global Knowledge Partnership on Migration and Development [KNOMAD] 2020) to support remittances led by Switzerland and the United Kingdom which was also motivated by the United Nation's International Day of Family Remittances.

This publication lays out 10 policy recommendations for development of digital remittances. We hope that these will

- help accelerate digital innovation in remittances,
- scale-up the benefits of digitization to migrant workers and their families, and
- continue to alleviate the remittance challenges of migrants and their families.

I would like to express my great appreciation to Junkyu Lee, Lisette Cipriano, and Jae Deuk Lee from the Finance Sector Group of the Sustainable Development and Climate Change Department; consultant Eric Van Zant; and Leon Isaacs and Poppy Isaacs from Developing Markets Associates for their invaluable contributions to this important publication.

**Bruno Carrasco**
Director General and concurrent Chief Compliance Officer
Sustainable Development and Climate Change Department
Asian Development Bank

# Acknowledgments

This publication was prepared as part of the support of the Asian Development Bank (ADB) to knowledge work on digital financial services among its developing member countries (DMCs). ADB continues to support the international community's Call to Action on Remittances launched in June 2020 to help migrant workers, their families, and the remittance industry badly hit by the coronavirus disease (COVID-19) pandemic. Policy makers supporting the development and scaling up of digital remittance channels will be crucial in building resiliency.

Lisette Cipriano, Senior Digital Technology Specialist (Financial Services), Sustainable Development and Climate Change Department (SDCC) led the effort to coordinate and contributed to the development and production of the publication. Background inputs in the publication were provided and assisted by Leon Isaacs, domain expert consultant on remittances. Junkyu Lee, Chief of Finance Sector Group, SDCC provided overall directions and supervised the production of the publication. In researching this publication, interviews were conducted for background context with central banks and government agencies, a range of industry experts. Publicly available documents were also accessed, including research reports, media articles, academic papers, webinars, and videos. ADB would like to thank all who have shared their expertise with us in this process. We would like to specially acknowledge support and insights from Dindo R. Santos, Director, Bangko Sentral ng Pilipinas; Eva Rosdiana Lase, Assistant Director, Bank of Indonesia; Zulfikar Ali Khokhar, Head Pakistan Remittances Initiative, State Bank of Pakistan; Shodi Sharifzoda, Specialist, Bakhtiyor Bahriddinov, Head of Statistics; and Sabokhat Zokirova, Head of Balance of Payments, Statistics and Balance of Payments Department, National Bank of Tajikistan. We also acknowledge Michael Davies, Darren Howells, and Tim Duston, Reserve Bank of New Zealand; and Rob Buchan, Director Pacific Operations, Australian Transaction Reports and Analysis Centre. Thank you also to Shiu Raj Singh, Financial Sector Specialist; Kelly Hattel, Senior Financial Sector Specialist; Mayumi Ozaki, Senior Financial Sector Specialist; Syed Ali-Mumtaz Shah, Principal Financial Sector Specialist; and Mohd Sani Moh Ismail, Principal Financial Sector Specialist, all of ADB, for facilitating these interviews.

Jae Deuk Lee, Financial Sector Specialist, SDCC; Shiu Raj Singh, Financial Sector Specialist, Pacific Department; and Poppy Isaacs, consultant, provided useful inputs and feedback. The publication was produced with the support of a team of ADB consultants comprising Eric Van Zant as editor; Monina Gamboa as proofreader; Joseph Manglicmot for typeset and layout; and Francis Manio for the graphics design of the cover. Katherine Mitzi Co, Associate Operations Analyst, SDCC and Raquel Borres, Senior Economics Officer, SDCC provided valuable administrative support.

The peer reviewers of this publication were Shiu Raj Singh, Financial Sector Specialist; Satoru Yamadera, Principal Financial Sector Specialist; Jonathan Grosvenor, Assistant Treasurer; and Syed Ali-Mumtaz Shah, Principal Financial Sector Specialist. We are most grateful for their feedback and advice. ADB greatly acknowledges all these contributions.

# Abbreviations

| | |
|---|---|
| ADB | Asian Development Bank |
| AML | anti-money laundering |
| CFT | countering financing of terrorism |
| COVID-19 | coronavirus disease 2019 |
| GDP | gross domestic product |
| GSMA | Global System for Mobile Communications Association |
| ID | identification |
| KYC | know your customer |
| PRC | People's Republic of China |
| SDG | Sustainable Development Goal |

# Introduction

**Remittances are a lifeline for many people in Asia and the Pacific.** They help families cover their day-to-day costs and invest in education, health, and small businesses, as well as represent a major source of foreign exchange for some of the developing member countries of the Asian Development Bank (ADB). In 2019, Asia was the largest remittance-receiving region in the world, at about $325 billion in formal remittances, or 45% of global flows (Global Knowledge Partnership on Migration and Development [KNOMAD] 2020).

**For a number of Asian countries, remittances account for a significant proportion of gross domestic product (GDP),** including Tonga (40%), Tajikistan (26%), the Kyrgyz Republic (25%), Nepal (23%), and Samoa (17%) (KNOMAD 2020).

**The international community has recognized the importance of remittances as a phenomenon for many years and has developed a number of global goals to address some of the challenges.** These include Sustainable Development Goal (SDG) 10.c, which targets that remittances cost no more than 3% by 2030 and that no single corridor costs more than 5% (the current average is 6.51%, quarter [Q] 4 2020, (World Bank 2020b).[1] In addition, the Global Compact for Safe and Orderly Migration Objective 20 aims to: "Promote faster, safer and cheaper transfer of remittances and foster financial inclusion of migrants" (United Nations 2019a).

**While the importance of remittances has been recognized globally, several challenges remain.** The price of sending remittances is particularly high in some parts of Asia and the Pacific, informal remittances that flow through *hawala* or *hundi* schemes are still high,[2] cash is still king in most markets, de-risking has meant some operators have been unable to get bank accounts, and some regulatory environments are too restrictive.

**Digitization can help address some of these challenges.** Digital services (including mobile money, online, and bank account credits) have long been recognized as the main solution to bring down remittance prices (a 2018 Global System for Mobile Communications Association [GSMA] study showed that international mobile money to mobile money service prices were only 1.7% in that year and were 3.51% in 2020 compared to 6.75% for the Remittance Prices Worldwide average) (GSMA 2018), increase access, provide more transparency, drive efficiency and help manage anti-money laundering (AML) and combating the financing of terrorism (CFT) risks.

**The coronavirus disease (COVID-19) pandemic has demonstrated the importance of a comprehensive and efficient digital remittance environment.** In many of the key sending and receiving countries, physical agent locations were closed during initial lockdown phases of the crisis. This often meant that those sending remittances were only able to use digital services, where they were available. A positive outcome has been the

---

[1]    World Bank (2020b). *COVID-19 Crisis through a Migration Lens. Migration and Development Brief 32.* Washington, DC: World Bank.

[2]    *Hawala* and *hundi* schemes are informal money transfer methods that operates through unauthorized service providers outside legal systems. It works through a trust system, with no money actually moving cross-border between the dealers. For the remittance sender and receiver, the process is similar to a formal service, as they approach a dealer with the money to send and are then normally provided with a code which they pass on to the receiver to collect the funds from the corresponding *hawala* dealer.

increased acceptance in some communities of the benefits of digital remittances as well as among providers that digital solutions must be offered. However, the rapid increase in the uptake of digital services has led to challenges; namely, how to introduce digitally driven solutions as quickly as possible to the people and areas where they are needed most. Digital and financial education are not widespread in rural communities.

This publication provides background on the importance of remittances to Asia, the challenges of remittances, the impact that the COVID-19 has had on remittances to Asia, two case studies of successful digitization programs in Asia, and recommendations for the way forward to digitize remittances.

# The Importance of Remittances to Asia

## Migration Patterns

The most common reason for migration is for work to support families back home. Asia is a diverse home to 4.6 billion people and many different cultures.[3] For migratory purposes, the region can be split into Central Asia, Pacific island countries, South Asia, and Southeast Asia. Migration is a common and important aspect of many people's lives in Asia. It was estimated that, in 2018, one in three migrants worldwide was from Asia (ADB 2018b).

**In 2019 the global stock of migrants from Asia was 84 million, representing the largest region of origin** (United Nations, Department of Economic and Social Affairs [UNDESA], 2019). Both in Asia and globally, India has the largest diaspora population (17.5 million emigrants), followed by the People's Republic of China (PRC) with 10.7 million emigrants (UNDESA 2019).[4] This is unsurprising given the size of the population. Outside of India and the PRC, the percentage of emigrants to home population is significant to a number of Asian countries, particularly Pacific island countries, for example, Tonga with 70% and Samoa with 63% (UNDESA 2020).[5] Figure 1 presents a clear picture of the percentage of migrants as a proportion of the home country population to demonstrate the prevalence of migration in a number of Asian countries.

**Asians are dispersed across the globe, as the range of migrant destination countries demonstrates.** Overall, the most popular region for Asian migrants is the Middle East. In 2018, close to 50% of migrants from South Asia (about 21 million) and 20% from Southeast Asia (about 4 million) migrated to the Middle East for economic purposes (ADB 2018b, Chapter 5). For migrants from Asia and the Pacific, the most popular destination countries are Australia, New Zealand, and the United States (US). In line with this, Australia is the host of the most migrants in Asia, reaching 7.1 million in 2017 (ADB 2018a, Chapter 5). Migration from Central Asia is mostly directed to the Russian Federation, due to historic ties.

**Intraregional migration is significant in Asia, with about 63% of Central and Southern Asian migrants originating from the region they migrate to**[6] (UNDESA 2019). India is a major host of Asian migrants, mostly from neighboring countries Bangladesh, Nepal, and Sri Lanka.

---

[3]   United Nations Department of Economic and Social Affairs (UNDESA). 2020. *Total Population.* https://population.un.org/wup/DataQuery/ (accessed 1 December 2020).

[4]   UNDESA. 2019. *International Migrant Stock by Destination and Origin.* https://www.un.org/en/development/desa/population/migration/data/ estimates2/estimates19.asp (accessed 1 December 2020).

[5]   UNDESA. 2019. *International Migrant Stock by Destination and Origin.* https://www.un.org/en/development/desa/population/migration/data/ estimates2/estimates19.asp (accessed 1 December 2020).

[6]   UNDESA (2019). *International migrant stock by destination and origin.*  Sourced 1.12.20

### Figure 1: Diaspora to Home Population

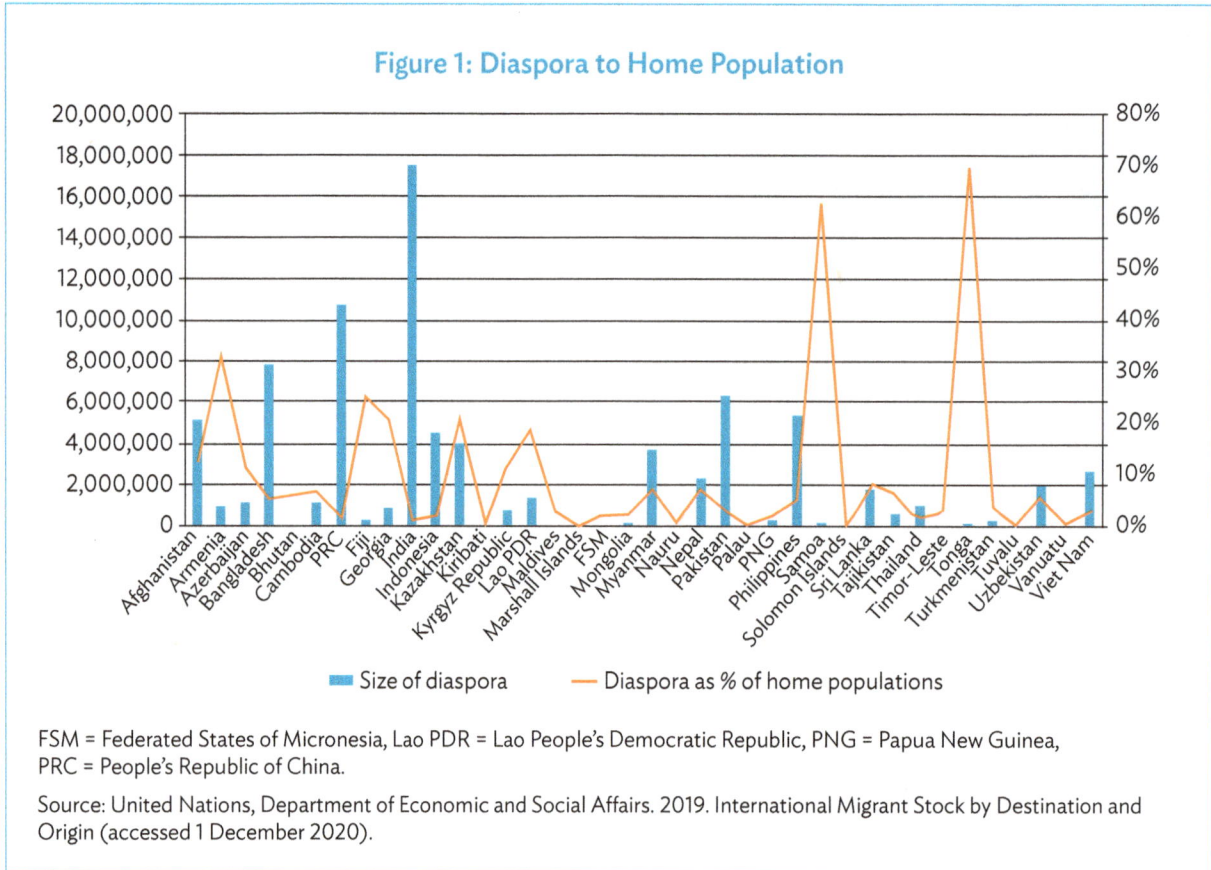

FSM = Federated States of Micronesia, Lao PDR = Lao People's Democratic Republic, PNG = Papua New Guinea, PRC = People's Republic of China.

Source: United Nations, Department of Economic and Social Affairs. 2019. International Migrant Stock by Destination and Origin (accessed 1 December 2020).

# Remittances

**Remittances are an important source of income, not only for the individuals receiving the funds, but also the country as a whole.** In 2019, Asia received $315 billion in remittances (ADB 2020), which makes it the largest remittance receiving region. By country, India is the largest receiver, totaling close to $80 billion, followed by the PRC, Pakistan, the Philippines, and Viet Nam. Figure 2 presents the remittance inflows to Asian countries, clearly showing South Asia as the top receiving subregion within Asia, at an estimated $140 billion in 2019 (World Bank 2019).

**Remittance patterns follow a similar trajectory to migration patterns with the Middle East being the top sending region to Asia**. Remittance flows from the Middle East predominantly go to South Asia and Southeast Asia. In 2018, India, Pakistan, and the Philippines received a total of $72.2 billion, which represented 75.8% of Middle East remittance outflows to Asia and 52.2% of the region's global outflows (Figure 2). Outside of the Middle East, the US is the largest individual sending country, reaching almost $72 billion in 2018 (World Bank 2019).

**Remittances are important for a large number of Asian countries as a percentage of gross domestic product (GDP)**. This is particularly relevant for Pacific developing member countries, for example, Tonga with 40%. Some Central Asian countries are also significantly reliant on remittances, such as Tajikistan (26%) and the Kyrgyz Republic (25%) (KNOMAD 2020).

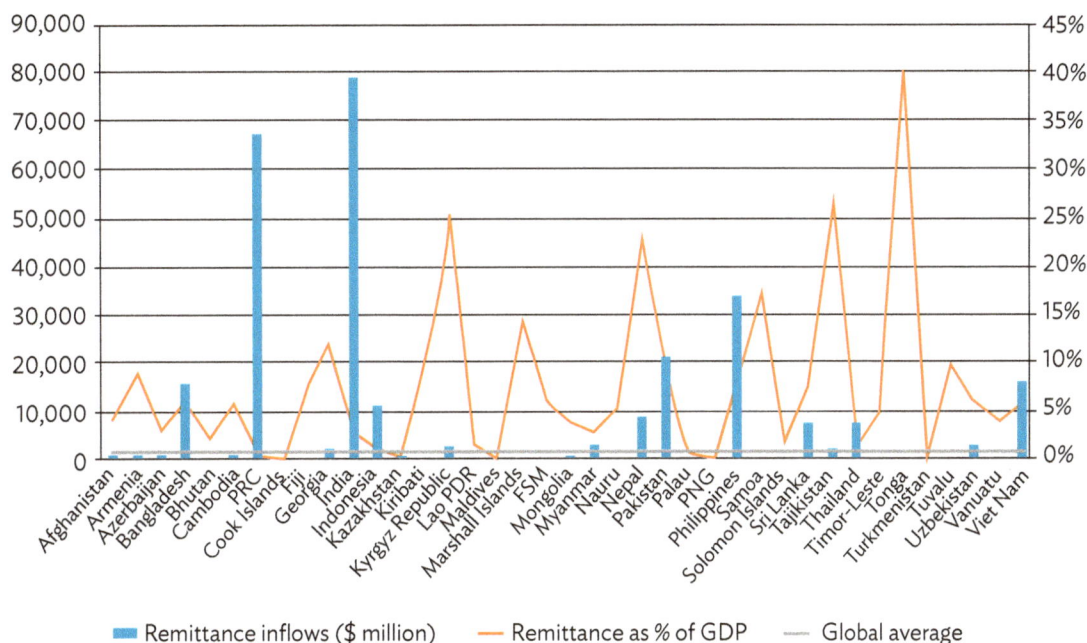

**Figure 2: Importance of Remittances to Asia**

Legend: ▬ Remittance inflows ($ million)  — Remittance as % of GDP  — Global average

FSM = Federated States of Micronesia, GDP = gross domestic product, Lao PDR = Lao People's Democratic Republic, PNG = Papua New Guinea, PRC = People's Republic of China.

Note: The blue bars are based on the Bilateral Remittance Matrix 2018.

Source: World Bank. 2018. Bilateral Remittance Matrix.

# Remittance Pricing

Remittance pricing across Asia varies, with no subregion reaching the SDG 10.c. target of 3% so far. Generally, sending remittances to Central Asia is cheapest and sending to Pacific island countries most expensive. Figure 3 presents the price of sending $200 (equivalent) to Asia in Q4 2020 against the global average of 6.51%, for countries with available data.[7] Notably, the COVID-19 pandemic may have impacted remittance prices in this iteration. Sending remittances to Central Asia is the cheapest because remittances are mostly sent from the Russian Federation, which are subject to no exchange rate since remittances are sent and received in rubles. The price is solely determined by the fee the operator charges. Remittances to Pacific island countries are expensive because of the small size of corridors, meaning a lack of competition. Additionally, the digital network to the islands is weak, meaning cash is dominant.

Remittance pricing is also determined by the sending country and the type of provider being used. For example, sending $200 cash from the Middle East to India averaged 3.71% in Q4 2020 and 3.29% to Sri Lanka, compared to sending the same amount from New Zealand to Samoa where the average was 11.62%.

---

[7]     Remittance pricing for the Cook Islands, the Federated States of Micronesia, Maldives, the Marshall Islands, Mongolia, Nauru, Palau, Timor-Leste, and Turkmenistan are unavailable.

## Figure 3: Remittance Price

**Average Price of Sending $200 to Asia**

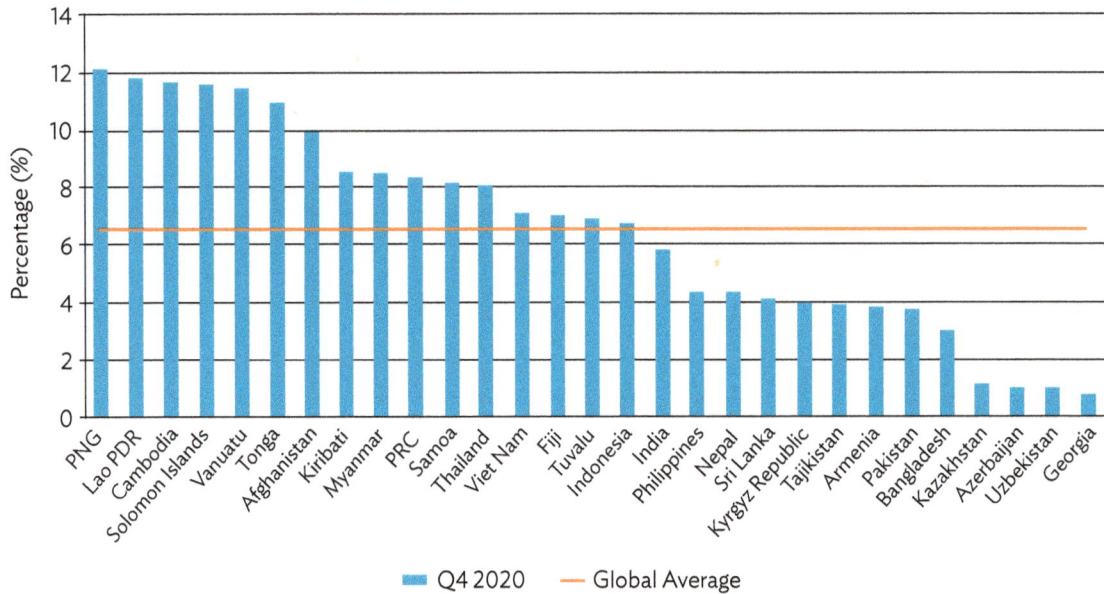

Lao PDR = Lao People's Democratic Republic, PNG = Papua New Guinea, PRC = People's Republic of China.

Sources: World Bank *Remittance Prices Worldwide* (accessed 1 December 2020) and SendMoneyPacific (accessed 1 December 2020).

# Challenges with Remittances

The importance of remittances and the benefit that they bring to millions of people is globally recognized. However, a number of significant challenges can make sending money home difficult.

## High Remittance Prices

**First, the high price of remittances remains a global challenge.** Remittances by definition are low-value transactions, most commonly sent on a regular basis by economic migrants to loved ones in their home country. The funds are largely used for basic consumption, such as food, bills, health care, education, and housing. However, the high price of remittances means that beneficiaries do not receive as much as they could. For example, if a Tongan migrant were to send $200 (equivalent) home and the price were 9.4% of the transaction, the receiver would essentially be losing nearly $19.

**Remittance prices across Asia vary, but are all above the global target SDG 10.c. on reducing the price to 3%.** A number of factors contribute to the high price of remittances, these include: a lack of competition; operational costs, particularly if it is a cash-to-cash service needing agents at both ends; compliance and know-your-customer (KYC) costs; de-risking and the sheer number of entities in the value chain (who all need to earn something and can include up to five different parties).[8]

**Sending money in cash is expensive.** This is largely due to the manual nature of this method: the sender goes to an agent and hands over cash, and the agent processes it, and the same actions take place on the receiving side. And bank transfers can be extremely expensive, a combination of bank fees plus the interbank exchange rate used makes for a costly transaction in some cases. For sending $200 (equivalent) from New Zealand to Kiribati, the price of sending through a bank ranges from 4.03% to 16.84% (SendMoneyPacific, Q4 2020).

**Sending remittances digitally is the cheapest and most efficient method.** Removing the costs of physical agents has often meant lower prices to the remittance sender and other significant benefits, such as accessibility in rural areas and aiding financial inclusion through the provision of accounts. However, as discussed later, cash still predominates in money transfers.

**A number of regulators, concerned with the high price of sending remittances, have introduced measures to reduce the price to senders and receivers.** For example, Bangladesh Bank has been offering 2% cash incentives to encourage Bangladeshi migrants to send money home to be paid out using banks, which are cheaper (Bangladesh Bank 2020). The value of remittances has been further recognized during the pandemic, with regulators introducing price reducing measures.

---

[8]  The five different parties involved in the traditional cash-to-cash remittance chain can include a sub-agent of the sending agent, the sending agent, the international money transfer operator, the paying-out agent, and the sub-agent of the paying-out agent. Potentially even more parties can be part of the value chain, including hub operators and so on.

# De-risking

**De-risking has been a significant problem for the remittance industry for nearly 10 years**. Under de-risking, banks terminate or restrict business relationships with a whole category of businesses, for example, money transfer operators, without taking into account the individual circumstances of the money transfer operator. As such, it is a blanket policy to avoid risk rather than manage it. And without their own business bank account, it is very hard for money transfer operators to operate at all or to protect their customers' money.[9] This began in around 2012 and has continued and evolved, largely driven by banks' lack of trust in the supervisory standards of the remittance sector.[10] In recent years, some money transfer operators (particularly those focused on a specific corridor) and agents of money transfer operators have seen their accounts closed and unable to open new ones in the Pacific island countries. The Reserve Bank of New Zealand (RBNZ) has focused on this issue and has recently encouraged banks to address the situation (RBNZ 2021).

**De-risking has had unintended consequences in the remittances market**, including, but not exclusive to, threatening progress in financial inclusion, reversing progress in reducing remittance prices and fees, the loss of access to financial services for humanitarian organizations, and pushing higher risk transactions from the regulated system into more opaque informal channels. This creates greater instability in the market.

**In recent years, central banks and other public sector organizations have taken some action to tackle the negative side effects of de-risking**. The Reserve Bank of New Zealand established the Pacific Remittance Project in 2019, with support from the Ministry of Foreign Affairs and Trade, to address de-risking challenges of the remittance market domestically and in the Pacific region. The project is still in early development and is a collective effort between the South Pacific Central Bank governors, the International Monetary Fund, and other agencies, to develop a regional KYC tool and approach, which would transform the remittance environment (Reserve Bank of Australia [RBA] 2020). Overall, the project seeks to enhance access to and reduce the price of remittances to and from the Pacific. It is also focused on increasing access to banking facilities and improving regulatory compliance. After obtaining approval for the second phase of the project, the Reserve Bank of New Zealand and partners will continue to develop the regional KYC facility and produce pan-regional guidance. As part of this program, ADB has supported the development of a KYC utility in Samoa. The utility is a central repository that stores the relevant data for KYC requirements. The utility will be established in collaboration with licensed money transfer operators, financial institutions, and regulators in Australia and New Zealand to ensure confidence in correspondent banking to Samoa. The pilot has received significant positive attention globally.

---

[9]  De-risking was driven from the United States, but impacts all countries, especially those that rely on US dollar trading. US dollar clearing banks, normally based in New York, have advised their international correspondents that they may not be able to offer their US dollar clearing services if the international bank continues to offer services to certain remittance customers. For example, money transfer operators that send money from Australia and the United Kingdom have been heavily impacted, while countries such as the Philippines have been impacted on the receiving end. Initially, the main reason behind the practice of de-risking was AML and CFT concerns. It has now expanded to cover banks' general concerns around profitability, but being justified as AML concerns.

[10]  See Financial Action Task Force publications on de-risking for more information (accessed 2 December 2020).

# Cash Is King

**Asia is considered a technology hub with the region having many digital payments options.** Cash, although expensive and inefficient, is still popular given the lack of alternative services. Digital services, including online and mobile, are becoming used more widely, but they are reliant on product availability, especially in rural areas, and creating awareness among users. Mobile money is available extensively in Africa, lowering prices and increasing access, but has not been as prominent in Asia (GSMA 2020b). Cash is still the dominant payment method for the majority of the population in Asia and the world as a whole.

**Cash remains dominant among remittance senders and receivers for several reasons.** These include the feeling of greater control over the transaction through giving cash to an agent or picking it up in person. Similarly, trust in the agent is a key factor in the remittance transaction—it is often easier to trust a person than a digital device. The study, PayPal (2017), found 57% of respondents preferred cash for day-to-day transactions. In the PRC; India; Hong Kong, China; Singapore; Thailand; the Philippines; and Indonesia, of 4,000 respondents asked how they preferred to receive money, more than 70% in India, Indonesia, and the Philippines said they used cash more often.

**A lack of financial education is a significant reason cash is still dominant (International Fund for Agricultural Development [IFAD] 2015).** It is an area where development agencies and banks are particularly keen to work. Remittance senders and participants have strong concerns over privacy, especially when providing personal details online. Extensive digital financial education is needed to alleviate some of the fears that people have over sending money online. The COVID-19 pandemic has been a catalyst for digital payments to grow.

# Informal Remittances

**Informal remittances are a global challenge in the remittance market.** These are transactions outside the formal financial system, and could include friends or family traveling with cash, bus drivers transporting cash across borders, or an organized informal provider (such as *hawala* or *hundi* operators). Another form of informal remittances is sending goods or services, for example buying televisions or white goods so a family can sell and get the money in local currency. By their nature, informal remittances are hard to quantify; some estimates suggest they are the equivalent of 50% higher than formal flows (Dilip Ratha 2011).

*Hawala/Hundi* **informal system is widely used in Asia (Rahman and Yeoh 2014).** People would choose to use these methods over the formal system for several reason. First, the price of formal transactions can be much higher than informal; KYC requirements may be unattainable for some migrant workers (documented or undocumented), and informal providers normally do not require any formal identification; recommendations from friends or family; and lack of financial education or awareness are also important. Informal providers carry considerable security risks.

**Naturally, regulators are concerned about informal remittance practices.** It is not possible to trace who is using them and foreign currency from them does not pass through formal channels, which has macroeconomic policy implications. But ultimately, people use informal transactions because they work. A key way to curb use of informal providers is, thus, to improve the ease and efficiency of formal remittance providers. This would include reducing the price of remittance transactions, harmonizing KYC regulations, and providing targeted and tailored financial education programs.

# Regulatory Environments

**Subregions differ significantly in their legal and regulatory frameworks**, which can be challenging for remittance service providers. Each country has its own policies, regulations, and agenda for money transfer. Greater harmonization of regulation would allow greater competition and allow policy makers to share best practice.

**It is difficult to harmonize regulation of technology and digital payments across the region**. It is a relatively new area with different countries at different stages of development. However, common standards in areas such as electronic know your customer (eKYC), fraud protection, and so on, would bring distinct benefits and faster adoption.

**The time it takes to approve license applications varies significantly across countries**. Although most countries have licensing regimes and processes, the private sector is concerned about the time to handle applications. Not only does it take longer to approve applications than is desirable, but some are concerned that very few countries publish timescales for a decision on an application. Best practice in this area includes provision of service level standards by regulators so that a known timescale is in place.

# Lack of Data

**Consistent and reliable data on remittances is lacking**. Although countries such as Bangladesh, Pakistan, and the Philippines have significantly improved data in recent years, with regular publishing of useful data, data is still lacking, especially data that would be helpful to remittance service providers and sometimes to remitters. Information on remittance inflows and outflows, method of sending or receiving, demographics (including gender, age, and location), among other things, would be very useful. Accurate data is crucial to understanding the importance of remittances to a home country.

# Impact of Coronavirus Disease on Remittances to Asia

**As coronavirus disease (COVID-19) became a global pandemic, many fear remittances were going to decline significantly**. In March 2020, the World Bank predicted that global remittance flows would decline 20% in 2020 (World Bank 2020b). The prediction has since been revised to a fall of 7%, to $508 billion in 2020, followed by a further decline of 7.5%, to $470 billion in 2021 for low- and middle-income countries (World Bank 2020a). In South Asia, the October 2020 predictions estimated a decline of 4% in 2020 and 11% in 2021. These declines would devastate the receivers of remittances relying on the money for their daily needs, although the actual figures for 2020 were not as severe as originally projected. Any decline in remittances to Asia could reverse decades of progress on poverty reduction, income inequality, nutrition, health, and education (World Economic Forum 2020).

**Economic lockdowns in the largest host countries, implemented to control the spread of COVID-19, caused the initial fears of remittance decline**. Much of Europe, the United States, and Gulf Cooperation Council countries had intense lockdowns lasting months. Migrants in host countries were more vulnerable to unemployment than nationals (World Bank 2020c), thus, migrants would have to send any savings, rather than wages. Furthermore, migrants without work, and therefore without visas, would have to return home, often without job prospects.

**Initially remittances declined to some Asian markets**. April saw major declines in nearly every market. For example, Bangladesh fell 25% (*The Financial Express* 2020), Sri Lanka fell 32% (Economynext 2020) and the Philippines (*Focus Economics* 2020) fell by 16% on year over year for that month.

**By the end of 2020, the impact was not as severe as initially predicted**. Indeed, remittances increased to some countries. In Bangladesh, the flow of inward remittances reached $19.8 billion in the full year 2020, up 8% year over year (KNOMAD 2020). Similarly, remittances to Pakistan reached $24.1 billion for full year 2020 (KNOMAD 2020), a 9% year-over-year rise. Personal remittances also remained strong to Fiji, with an increase of 11% in the year, equivalent to $653 million (*Fiji Village* 2021).

**Volumes did not fall as severely as predicted for several reasons**. These include travel restrictions leading to informal remittances switching to formal, government efforts, and changes in customer behavior. People were unable to travel so could not hand-carry money. Also, *hawala* operators, who often settle their payments by shipping cash on planes, were not able to do so. Secondly, Saudi Arabia is the largest sending market from the Gulf, and the authorities announced that, due to the pandemic, people from outside the Saudi Arabia could not travel to perform Hajj in 2020. Money usually spent on the pilgrimage was sent home instead. Remittance flows from Saudi Arabia to Pakistan reached $3.3 billion from July to November 2020. A third reason is some favorable exchange rates leading to migrants remitting additional funds, as in the case of the Nepali rupee against the US dollar in July 2020.[11]

---

[11]    The Nepali rupee depreciated by 9.2% in July 2020 compared to 0.02% in July 2019.

**Central Banks introduced initiatives to encourage migrants to send money home**. Incentives included a reduction in transfer fees or increasing daily transaction limits. Pakistan waived all charges for using online transfer services into the country (State Bank of Pakistan 2020). In Bangladesh, a bonus payment of 2% of the transfer value was introduced for receipt of formal remittances (Bangladesh Bank 2020).

**Migrants have made every effort to continue sending remittances**. Resilient migrants have found successful ways to continue to earn money so they can send remittances. They have also used savings. Evidence from operators indicate that the average value of a transaction decreased, but the frequency of sending increased.

**While COVID-19 has been devastating for many people, it has also catalyzed change in the remittances market**. Digital remittance services have become more important during the pandemic for many remittance senders and receivers.[12] For example, Western Union, MoneyGram, and Ria Money annual returns to their respective markets have shown a doubling volume of digital remittances (Table 1).

### Table 1: Digital Transactions Made through Money Transfer Operators 2020–2021

| Company | Increase in Transactions 2020 | Percent of Total Transactions | |
|---|---|---|---|
| | | 2021 | 2020 |
| Western Union | 94% | 28% | 16% |
| MoneyGram | 80% | 29% | 16% |
| Ria | >100% | Not available | |

Sources: Western Union Annual Report 2020. https://s21.q4cdn.com/100551446/files/doc_financials/2020/ar/2020-Annual-Report-2021-Proxy-Statement.pdf; MoneyGram results for 2020. https://ir.moneygram.com/node/21586/pdf; Euronet/Ria Annual results 2020: https://ir.euronetworldwide.com/news-releases/news-release-details/euronet-worldwide-reports-fourth-quarter-and-full-year-2020.

Because money transfer operators were not initially considered essential services in a number of key host countries, traditional cash options were limited. This forced people to switch their sending instrument to digital, mostly from the send side. One of the key issues to address to persuade migrants to use digital services is the fear of online fraud or scams, or not understanding the process in general. However, once someone successfully performs a digital transaction, they are unlikely to revert to cash.

**Digital remittance service options have increased significantly since the beginning of the pandemic**. Many operators offered incentives, or simply information to switch or attract customers to digital. In Asia, the use of apps and online sending services increased. There were also innovations such as a recently announced agreement between the blockchain payments provider, Ripple, Mobile Money (the Malaysian mobile wallet provider), and bKash (the mobile money provider in Bangladesh) (PYMNTS.com 2021).

**It is difficult to quantify the increase of digital remittances for 2020 to Asia as a whole due to a lack of data collection in this area**. However, some individual central banks record remittance transactions and have seen an increase from the previous year (2019) in the use of digital services. The Central Bank of Tajikistan said that

---

[12]    Digital remittances should be defined as services that use digital methods at both the sending and receiving ends of transaction. Frequently, remittance service providers define a digital transaction as one where digital is used on at least one end, for examples, online sending to cash receiving, or cash at the sending end to mobile wallet at the receiving end.

throughout 2020 digital remittance transactions to Tajikistan increased 24.7% as a result of digital initiatives,[13] while Pakistan saw an increase in transactions of 26% (State Bank of Pakistan 2021) and Bangladesh saw an upswing of 8% (*The Daily Star* 2021).

**Other central banks actively encouraged people to use digital payments**. The Bangko Sentral ng Pilipinas introduced two clearinghouses: the Philippine Electronic Fund Transfer System and Operations Network PESONet and InstaPay for digital transactions. InstaPay allows transactions worth ₱50,000 or less to be credited in real-time. PESONet allows funds of higher value to be sent and credited on the same day. Use of PESONet and InstaPay increased throughout the pandemic. A number of banks waived transfer fees for using these services. The central bank also postponed charges for fund transfers made through the Philippine Payment and Settlement System until the end of 2021, to encourage digital payments. The value of transactions through InstaPay rose almost 400%, and PESONet rose 100% year over year.[14] While this domestic infrastructure encourages Filipinos to use digital payments, notably, it only indirectly impacts the inflow of cross-border remittances. This is discussed in the Philippines case study below (Box 1).

---

[13]   Sourced from interviews with the Central Bank of Tajikistan in February 2020.
[14]   Sourced from interviews with Philippines stakeholders.

# Digitization and Remittances

Digital remittances have been heralded as a key enabler for achieving global remittance targets. In particular:

- Digitization can bring a number of benefits, namely reducing transfer prices, and improving transparency, efficiency, convenience, and access:
  » The Global System for Mobile Communications or GSM Association (commonly referred to as GSMA), the trade body for the mobile operators, has undertaken market surveys to determine the prices of sending money through mobile services compared to other methods. The data show that the price to send money from mobile wallet to another mobile wallet internationally was 3.53% in Q3 2020 compared to the global average for sending remittances which was 6.75% (Remittance Prices Worldwide) (GSMA 2020a).
  » Digital remittances normally result in the crediting of money to an account. Account holders can then use remittances to pay for multiple products. Some of these products may have a cost attached (such as cashing out), but these costs are not included in remittance calculations because it is the account holder's choice whether to incur these costs or not.
  » Even where money is sent digitally to an account or a wallet and the consumer wishes to withdraw cash, the price is still lower than a traditional cash-to-cash remittance (GSMA and World Bank) because the send end of the transaction does not need an agent.[15]
- Digital financial services can boost the resilience of the financial sector, especially during crises. This is done by reducing prices, increasing convenience, reducing the time spent sending money, and increasing access. Senders and receivers do not need to leave home to make or receive money.

In total, international remittances via mobile money contribute to 14 of the 17 SDGs (Figure 4). Because of its reach and growing use among underserved people, mobile money is uniquely positioned to transform formal remittance markets and to advance financial inclusion. Mobile money providers are at the forefront of domestic payment services in many emerging markets, enabling the recipients of international remittances to pay for goods and services digitally, in turn creating a payments history that could enable them to access credit or insurance in the future. Mobile money has thus established itself as a critical tool for facilitating international remittances, while reducing remittance prices and maximizing the impact of remittances on development.

---

[15] Any payment that involves an agent will result in a higher price for to the consumer. See https://www.developingmarkets.com/sites/default/files/Supply%20and%20Demand%2015-03-2010.pdf. https://www.fsdafrica.org/wp-content/uploads/2019/08/Scaling-up-Remittances-15.06.2017_Final-1.pdf for more information.

**Figure 4: Contribution of Mobile Money to the Sustainable Development Goals**

Source: Global System for Mobile Communications Association. 2019. *Harnessing the power of mobile money to achieve SDGs.* https://www.gsma.com/mobilefordevelopment/wp-content/uploads/2019/10/GSMA-Harnessing-the-power-of-mobile-money-to-achieve-the-SDGs.pdf.

# Three Case Studies: Philippines, Malaysia, Pakistan

Examples from the Philippines, Malaysia, and Pakistan provide insights into what can be done to improve the environment for remittances by using digital payments (Boxes 1, 2, and 3). In the Philippines, a key lesson is that by improving the domestic payments environment, international remittances can benefit. More broadly, better domestic payment systems can encourage more people to obtain accounts and become "financially included," removing their need to receive money in cash. On a practical level, improved domestic payment systems can lead to faster straight-through processing of receiving transactions to accounts, which increases speed and lowers prices.

The importance of digitization to addressing many of the challenges with remittances cannot be overstated. When properly deployed they help reduce the price of remittances, increase access for consumers, address gender issues, improve settlement, optimize operations, provide valuable data, and many other benefits.

## Box 1: Philippines

**The Philippines has a coherent payments digitization strategy.** The Bangko Sentral ng Pilipinas (BSP), the central bank, introduced the "Digital Payments Transformation Roadmap," which outlines a series of initiatives to transition, and increase, digital payments to 50% of all payments by 2023 and aims to increase financial inclusion to 70%, also by 2023. The strategic outcomes include stronger customer preference for digital payments, and more innovative and responsive digital financial services.

**Prior to introducing the road map, the number of Filipinos with any form of account, bank or otherwise, was low.** Data from Findex suggests that only 34% of the adult population had an account in 2017.[a] The popularity of cash, varying socioeconomic levels due to geography, and the lack of financial inclusion were the reasons behind the low number.

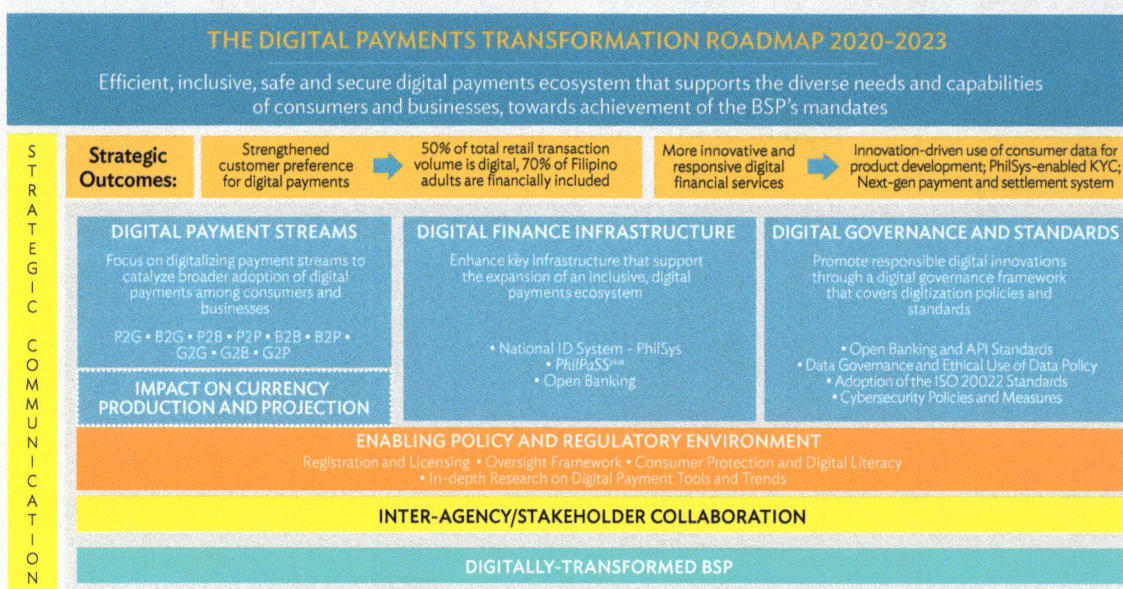

B2B = business-to-business, B2G = business-to-government, B2P = business-to-person, G2B = government-to-business, G2G = government-to-government, G2P = government-to-person, ID = identification, KYC = know your customer, P2B = person-to-business, P2G = person-to-government, P2P = person-to-person.

Source: Bangko Sentral ng Pilipinas. *Philippines Digital Payments Transformation Roadmap.*

**The road map's three pillars for successful transition to digital payments are as follows:**
- Digital payment streams: Create compelling and large-scale digital payments use cases. These include all use cases, such as government-to-person and person-to-person.
- Create digital finance infrastructure that is secure, reliable, efficient, and interconnected for smooth payment transactions. Interoperability is a key component of this. In the Philippines, this includes InstaPay (which is the current instant payment stream) and PESONet (a batched payment stream). An interoperable system will allow smooth transactions.
- Digital governance and standards aligned with global best practices and standards to ensure provision of digital products and services are covered by an adequate governance process (BSP). The last pillar also includes increasing customer confidence in digital services.

**A supporting feature is the introduction of a digital national identification (ID) scheme.** This will support the payment system and will facilitate real-time processing of financial transactions. In addition, the National QR Code Standard (QR Ph) was introduced in November 2019 to accelerate progress of digital payments. The QR code contains important information relating to an account, such as the account name and number, enabling use for retail payments and greater speed and efficiency. BSP wants to expand from peer-to-peer to person-to-merchant, so that small businesses that may not have an account can accept payments digitally.

[a] World Bank. 2017. Global Financial Inclusion (Global FINDEX) Database 2017. https://globalfindex.worldbank.org/ (accessed 13 January 2021).

Source: Authors.

## Box 2: Valyou in Malaysia

Between 2017 and 2020, the Global System for Mobile Communications Association (GSMA) conducted the study *How Mobile Money is Scaling International Remittances and Fostering Financial Resilience: Learnings from Valyou in Malaysia.* Traditionally, sending remittances from Malaysia to those two countries has been cash-based and often informal (using the *hawala* system). The Malaysian mobile money provider, Valyou, piloted an app-based international remittance service for migrant workers from Bangladesh and Pakistan. The pilot revealed that mobile money can help turn informal flows into formal, reduce remittance prices, and increasing financial inclusion and uptake by female recipients.

The figure details a high-level overview of the outcomes of the pilot.

### GSMA/Valyou Pilot Outcomes

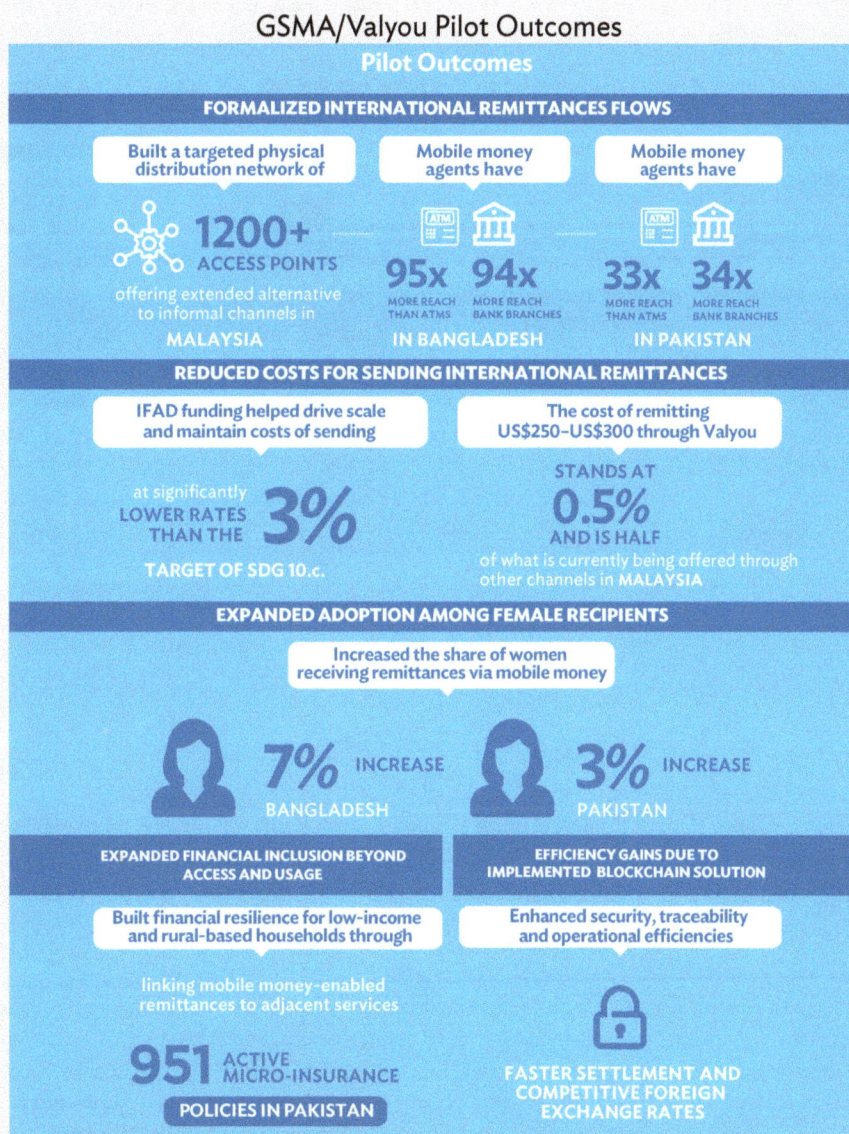

**Pilot Outcomes**

**FORMALIZED INTERNATIONAL REMITTANCES FLOWS**

Built a targeted physical distribution network of
**1200+** ACCESS POINTS
offering extended alternative to informal channels in **MALAYSIA**

Mobile money agents have
**95x** MORE REACH THAN ATMS    **94x** MORE REACH BANK BRANCHES
**IN BANGLADESH**

Mobile money agents have
**33x** MORE REACH THAN ATMS    **34x** MORE REACH BANK BRANCHES
**IN PAKISTAN**

**REDUCED COSTS FOR SENDING INTERNATIONAL REMITTANCES**

IFAD funding helped drive scale and maintain costs of sending
at significantly LOWER RATES THAN THE **3%** TARGET OF SDG 10.c.

The cost of remitting US$250–US$300 through Valyou
STANDS AT **0.5%** AND IS HALF of what is currently being offered through other channels in **MALAYSIA**

**EXPANDED ADOPTION AMONG FEMALE RECIPIENTS**

Increased the share of women receiving remittances via mobile money
**7%** INCREASE **BANGLADESH**
**3%** INCREASE **PAKISTAN**

**EXPANDED FINANCIAL INCLUSION BEYOND ACCESS AND USAGE**

Built financial resilience for low-income and rural-based households through
linking mobile money-enabled remittances to adjacent services
**951** ACTIVE MICRO-INSURANCE **POLICIES IN PAKISTAN**

**EFFICIENCY GAINS DUE TO IMPLEMENTED BLOCKCHAIN SOLUTION**

Enhanced security, traceability and operational efficiencies
**FASTER SETTLEMENT AND COMPETITIVE FOREIGN EXCHANGE RATES**

ATM = automated teller machine, IFAD = International Fund for Agricultural Development, SDG = Sustainable Development Goal.

Source: Global System for Mobile Communications Association. 2021. *How mobile money is scaling international remittances and fostering financial resilience: Learnings from Valyou Malaysia.*

*continued on next page*

*Box 2: continued*

**A key outcome if the Valyou pilot is formalization of remittances flows**. By leveraging their existing relationships with the Bangladeshi local telco, Digi, and partnering with mom-and-pop shops, Valyou was able to set up a targeted distribution network, significantly aiding higher formal remittance transactions. Customers in Bangladesh are also able to receive remittances directly into a mobile money account, which has helped increase convenience, particularly for those in rural areas who would have to travel to their nearest money transfer operator.

**Consumer behavior changed in Pakistan by incentivizing consumers to remit funds through the mobile money app**. The price of remitting was significantly lower than the 3% global target. To achieve this, Valyou concentrated on reducing business costs in physical locations. The pilot focused on migrating customers from the more costly method of sending cash via an agent to remitting through a mobile app which has a lower price. By incentivizing people to use a mobile money app, the pilot reduced physical remittance prices threefold and kept remittance prices below 3%. As a result, Valyou's business model changed from 99% cash at an agent to only 35%.

**Financial inclusion and financial education increased among female recipients**. In Pakistan, 82% of women, and in Bangladesh, 64% of women were financially excluded in 2019 (Women's World Banking 2020). One of the focuses of the pilot was to improve financial inclusion among women. In Bangladesh, 50% of customers using the app-based service were women. While financial inclusion did improve for women in Pakistan, uptake was lower than in Bangladesh.

**Innovative measures such as a blockchain-enabled remittance service were used**. This was specifically between Malaysia and Pakistan. It was a major help in addressing ID concerns and by using a decentralized blockchain approach to identity greater security was achieved in this important area. Blockchain also helped to deliver faster settlement, greater operational efficiencies, and more competitive foreign exchange rates.

**The study notes that regulating remittances is difficult and time-consuming**. This is especially true when considering that multiple countries are involved, which means multiple regulations and different geographies. However, the Valyou study concludes that if regulators are "willing to explore new routes or new tools to enhance traditional financial activities," the results will be greater financial inclusion.[a]

[a] GSMA. 2020a. *How Mobile Money Is Scaling International Remittances and Fostering Financial Resilience: Learnings from Valyou in Malaysia.*
[b] Women's World Banking. Bangladesh. https://www.womensworldbanking.org/country-strategies-bangladesh/.
Source: Authors.

## Box 3: Pakistan

The Pakistan Remittance Initiative was launched in August 2009 as a joint program between the State Bank of Pakistan, the Ministry of Overseas Pakistanis and Human Resource Development, and the Ministry of Finance to facilitate and support safer, cheaper, convenient, and efficient flows of remittances through formal channels and create investment opportunities in Pakistan for overseas Pakistanis.

The initiative has adopted a truly multifaceted approach which covers every area of remittances, including: expansion of outreach to diaspora, pre-departure briefings for emigrants, enhancement of distribution channels (including post offices and microfinance institutions), improvements in payment system infrastructure (including digital payments), educating banks and others to introduce new products. Most importantly, it covers subsiding the fees that would normally be paid by receivers by giving money to pay-out banks to share with sending businesses for all transactions over $100 on condition that no fee is charged to the sender or receiver and that the foreign exchange margin is capped at 1% maximum. The approach has clearly worked in the long term (see figure): figure highlights how overall volumes have risen from $8 billion when the program started to $24 billion in 2020[a]

*continued on next page*

*Box 3: continued*

## Growth of Inbound Remittances to Pakistan 2001 to 2020

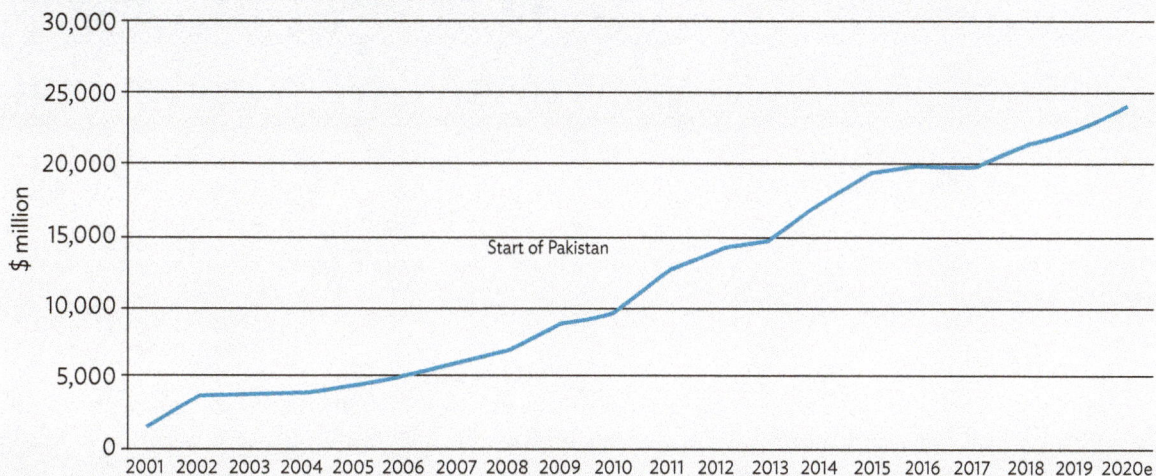

*$ million* (y-axis), values: 0, 5,000, 10,000, 15,000, 20,000, 25,000, 30,000

Label on chart: "Start of Pakistan"

x-axis: 2001 2002 2003 2004 2005 2006 2007 2008 2009 2010 2011 2012 2013 2014 2015 2016 2017 2018 2019 2020e

Source: Global Knowledge Partnership on Migration and Development (KNOMAD). 2020. Remittance inflows https://www.knomad.org/data/remittances?page=1.

Digital enhancements have played an increasingly important role in the further development of remittances in Pakistan. The country has taken a holistic approach driven by the National Payments Strategy, which was launched in 2019. It is all-encompassing action for multiple stakeholders from the public and private sectors (State Bank of Pakistan [SBP] 2019).[b]

Many steps are encouraging faster adoption of digital payments including licensing entities to offer mobile payments, mwallet scheme to encourage sending money directly to a mobile wallet, prepaid Pakistan Remittance Initiative cards, biometrically verified identification, and improved domestic settlement system, including the Automatic Direct Clearing/Internet Bank Fund Transfer (ACH IBFT) system, biometric-based ATM withdrawals, and others. Early evidence shows that these initiatives are working. For example, prior to the coronavirus disease (COVID-19) pandemic, the ACH IBFT was handling around 180,000 transactions per day and by the end of 2020 this had increased to 800,000.[c]

One other key recent example is the Roshan Digital account. This is an initiative of the SBP. It enables Non-resident Pakistanis to open accounts from wherever they are in the world. Once open (usually within 48 hours) the account holder can send money into them and undertake multiple banking functions such as payments and investments. The initiative had a key benefit to holders, namely that the funds are repatriable so that they can be used abroad with no restrictions.[d]

The initiative was launched in September 2020 and in its first 6 months it has received over $671 million. It has been heavily promoted and is well received.

This is another example of a fully integrated and long-term commitment to improve remittances. Crucially, the State Bank undertakes regular surveys of remittance senders and receivers to understand which services are most attractive for them.

[a] KNOMAD. 2020. Remittance inflows https://www.knomad.org/data/remittances?page=1.
[b] State Bank of Pakistan. 2019. *National Payment System Strategy*. https://www.sbp.org.pk/ps/PDF/NPSS.pdf.
[c] Based on stakeholder interviews with the State Bank of Pakistan.
[d] Based on stakeholder interviews with the State Bank of Pakistan.

Source: Authors.

# ADB Support for Remittances

ADB has actively supported remittance initiatives and has driven a number of projects that link remittances to digitization. These include

- Supporting of the KYC utility in Samoa as outlined previously (IMF 2020);
- Promoting Remittance for Development Finance "Digital Payment Systems, Mobile Money Services, and Agent Banking, Bangladesh, Nepal, and Sri Lanka" (ADB 2016). This was a technical assistance report; and
- "Bangladesh: Institutional Support for Migrant Workers 2010–16" (ADB 2017). This was originally conceived to issue at least 18,000 debit cards to rural clients for remittance transactions to help reduce informal remittance transactions. However, the scope of the grant was significantly changed to finance a real-time gross payment instead as a result of a greater understanding of the remittances environment and because of some technical matters relating to the grant facility.[16]

ADB can play a major role in helping to change the landscape for the remittances and digital payments environment within Asia by providing research and dialogue leadership on the topic and also strategic funding to help nations develop scalable solutions that could be applied to multiple countries across the region. Aside from some technical elements in how grants are awarded, the other key lesson learned from the above program to take forward is that it is imperative to be pragmatic about what can be achieved and to fully understand the entire environment for remittances and payments for all stakeholders. Thus, commissioning an independent scoping assessment report prior to the beginning of a project is an essential prerequisite.

---

[16] The project was evaluated as partly satisfactory because the real-time gross payment system was implemented effectively, but the volume of remittances via informal operators actually increased. These two elements were not connected.

# Recommendations

2020 saw a dramatic increase in the use of digital remittances worldwide. As a result of the global pandemic, sending money digitally was often the only option to send remittances. However, while there has been an increase in digital transactions, cash remains the predominant method of money transfer. To increase the use of digital remittances, the recommendations listed here could aid in transitioning people from cash to digital.

The recommendations have been divided based on the type of entity that should be responsible for leading each one, ADB, national governments/regulators, or the private sector. Naturally, many of the recommendations will require multistakeholder action. Within each section, the recommendations have, where possible, been ordered to reflect their importance.

It is envisaged that, given the number of countries and the differing circumstances throughout ADB's developing member countries, that many of the recommendations will occur in parallel. Some recommendations will be more relevant for some countries than others, depending on the levels of digital capacity and regulatory frameworks.

A logical first step would be for each country to determine its current position to determine which of the recommendations is most appropriate for them and in which order.

## To be driven by the Asian Development Bank

### Country digital remittances tool kit
Developing a structured and consistent approach to implementing digital remittance solutions would bring value to all countries in Asia where remittances are important. Each country is at a different stage of digital development and has specific local circumstances. However, consistent elements need to be addressed to implement digital remittances effectively, such as infrastructure, identification, AML/CFT, regulations for market participants, linkage to foreign exchange, innovation approaches, and so on. The creation of a tool kit based on practical experiences which allows a country to benchmark its current situation and develop a practical road map on how to reach its goals would be a highly valuable tool.

### Enhance digital capacity and improve remittance-related policies and practices
Countries within Asia are at different levels in their development of remittance markets and environments. ADB has an important role in assisting with building digital capacity, helping with regulations, and providing practical guidance to many countries. ADB will bring the lessons it has learned in other projects it has funded. This will help increase consistency and drive sustainable gains.

### Increase regional cooperation including sharing best practice

Asia has a wide variety of environments for remittances. Regular discussions with all stakeholders have revealed a need to create vehicles to enable enhanced sharing of knowledge. This can help improve cooperation between countries. Examples of actions that have been taken and evidence-based decision-making would be highly appreciated. Potential solutions include an Asia-wide remittances information portal, webinars, conferences, and discussion groups.

## To be driven by governments, including regulators and supervisors

### Increase financial education in digital services

An important way to increase digital transactions is to educate people on the benefits of it. Research has shown a significant gap between men and women in levels of financial education, favoring men, particularly in rural areas (Sholevar and Harris 2020). Digital remittances can help bridge this gap. Customers can access digital remittances from their smartphone, tablet, or laptop. The latest figures suggest that 35% of the world has access to a smartphone (Review 42 2020).

The responsibility of increasing financial education falls to all entities involved in the remittance transaction. Regulators can ensure that pre-departure training is offered, or made compulsory, for migrants before they leave to a host country. National financial education strategies can be expanded to include digital remittances. Money transfer operators can offer advice to senders and receivers of remittances at agent stores. International organizations, such as the International Organization for Migration and International Labour Organization, have been involved in increasing financial education through developing training packages for localized financial education. While these traditionally include training on spending, budgeting, and various financial products, they could also be expanded to include specific information of digital remittances.

### Use of technology to support anti-money laundering and countering financing of terrorism regulations

AML/CFT is critical for the long-term benefit of the economy and finance as a whole for all countries. Concern exists, however, that some measures used to enforce it may damage access to services for individuals (e.g., with limited ID) and lead to an increase in remittance prices as remittance service providers need to implement more expensive controls to manage it. However, the effective management of AML/CFT regulations and activities can really strengthen the reputation of a country by influencing de-risking activities by banks and reducing informal transactions, among other areas.

Judicious use of technology could be a suitable solution to AML/CFT concerns, and solutions should be examined. For example, the National Bank of Rwanda "pulls" data directly from the information technology systems of more than 600 supervised financial institutions, including commercial banks, insurance companies, microfinance institutions, pension funds, forex bureaus, telecom operators, and money transfer operators. This delivers timely, consistent, and reliable data to the National Bank of Rwanda. It has also led to improvements in financial institutions' data, which they now also use for internal risk management (Bank for International Settlements 2018).

### Interoperability

Interoperability would mean that remittance service providers, banks, and mobile money can send and receive remittances across different networks. Having an integrated payments infrastructure leads to fair access to market players. This, in turn, will create more affordable and efficient transactions. All around, it would make sending remittances a much more seamless process. Furthermore, with an interoperable system there will be a greater opportunity for effective risk management, as everyone will be on the same system, thus increasing transparency.

However, creating an interoperable environment will be challenging without collaboration among stakeholders. For effective interoperability, legal frameworks, and business models and policies must be harmonized. Some East African countries have had success with interoperable mobile networks, particularly Tanzania (GSMA 2016). These can be emulated in Asia.

### Development of digital identification solutions

Electronic national identification (ID) cards have been introduced in a number of Asian countries. India has been leading the way in Asia and many countries have followed, such as Indonesia, Thailand, and more recently, the Philippines. Overall, digital ID can be a gateway to greater financial inclusion for many. The benefits to having a digital ID include reducing the threat of identity fraud and saving time in authentication, thereby increasing efficiency. A digital ID could enable verification and authentication from a device.

## To be driven by the private sector

### Incentivize digital transactions

Migrants and recipient family members are often hesitant to try digital transactions, for a number of reasons. Fear of fraud and scams are key causes of anxiety for remittance senders and receivers. By providing monetary, or other incentives to people, they are more inclined to try the service. Both regulators and money transfer operators have been offering incentives to send remittances digitally throughout the pandemic, which has contributed to the uptake. Numerous demand-side studies have also found that once customers try digital services, they are unlikely to go back to their previous method of transfer.

### Simplify on-boarding while reassuring that it is secure

Signing up to digital services can often be daunting for migrants. Having to provide personal information, such as account information and ID number, can cause fear of fraud and scams. Making the on-boarding process simple, at the same time as reassuring them that it is secure, will be essential to converting people to digital services. Tailoring on-boarding to migrants is a first step, rather than just creating a "one-size-fits-all" approach. Quick turnaround of approval is needed.

## For all

### Regulators, financial institutions, and money transfer operators should work together to safeguard remittances and promote competition and innovation

With the private sector developing innovative approaches to cross-border payments, regulators could create an enabling environment for the use of new technology, and at the same time minimize money-laundering risks (IFC 2016). In regulation, an enabling policy framework is needed to provide clear, consistent, and predictable legal provisions for remittances, a proportionate risk-based approach for KYC/customer due diligence, assurance of data protection, security and privacy, transparency, and competition within the market, and finally, the acceptance of the use of technology to be used for transactions. Supervision and oversight is also needed. A review of legal and regulatory frameworks that presents any barriers to the use of digital channels (Alliance for Financial Inclusion 2018).

In infrastructure, robust retail payments and financial systems are needed. This includes cash-in-cash-out networks and national retail payment systems. The national retail payment systems need to be able to connect with international payment hubs and gateways. Strong, comprehensive infrastructure for identification is also needed.

# Key Messages

Remittances are a lifeline for many people in Asia and the Pacific. They help families cover their day-to-day costs and invest in education, health, and small businesses, and are a source of foreign exchange for governments. In 2019, Asia was the largest remittance-receiving region in the world, at about $325 billion in formal remittances, or 45% of global flows. By country, India is the largest receiver, totaling close to $80 billion, followed by the PRC, the Philippines, Pakistan, and Viet Nam. For a number of Asian countries, remittances account for a significant proportion of GDP, including Tonga (40%), Tajikistan (26%), the Kyrgyz Republic (25%), Nepal (23%) and Samoa (17%) (KNOMAD 2020).

Remittance pricing across Asia varies, with no subregion reaching the SDG 10.c. target of 3%. Generally, sending remittances to Central Asia is cheapest and to Pacific island countries, most expensive.

Several challenges inhibit optimum growth of remittances globally and in the region, including the high price of sending remittances in some parts of Asia and the Pacific (especially as cash is the most popular method used), high levels of informal remittances that flow through the *hawala* or *hundi* schemes, de-risking has meant some operators have been unable to get bank accounts, some regulatory environments are too restrictive, and timely, accurate, or published data are often lacking.

Coronavirus disease (COVID-19) had a major impact on remittances in Asia. In many of the key sending and receiving countries, physical agent locations were closed during initial lockdown phases of the crisis and some feared that global remittance numbers might fall by as much as 20%. In reality, the fall over the whole year was not as much as feared, with a number of countries demonstrating real growth. However, the picture was not uniform and certainly, during Q2, there were significant drops.

The COVID-19 pandemic demonstrated the importance of a comprehensive and efficient digital remittance environment to address not only the impact of COVID-19, but also the broader challenges facing remittances. Digital services (including mobile money, online and bank account credits) have long been recognized as the main solution to bring down remittance prices, increase access, provide more transparency, drive efficiency, and help manage AML/CFT risks. In fact, in total, international remittances via mobile money contributed to 14 of the 17 SDGs.

The COVID-19 crisis led to an increase in digital transactions, but cash is still predominant. To increase use of digital remittances, a series of recommendations has been developed that could help move people from cash to digital. Each country will need to review its own circumstances and develop locally appropriate solutions. ADB can play a catalytic role.

#### Table 2: Recommended Actions to Increase Digital Remittances

| No. | Recommendation |
|-----|----------------|
| **For Asian Development Bank** | |
| 1 | Country digital remittances tool kit |
| 2 | Enhance digital capacity and improve remittance-related policies and practices |
| 3 | Increase regional cooperation including the sharing best practice |
| **For governments, including regulators and regulators** | |
| 4 | Increase financial education on digital services |
| 5 | The use of technology to support AML and CFT regulations |
| 6 | Interoperability |
| 7 | Development of digital ID solutions |
| **For private sector** | |
| 8 | Incentivize digital transactions |
| 9 | Simplify on-boarding process, while reassuring that it is secure |
| **For all** | |
| 10 | Regulators, financial institutions, and money transfer operators should work together to safeguard remittances and promote competition and innovation |

AML = anti-money laundering, CFT = countering financing of terrorism, ID = identification.
Source: Authors.

Capacity and desire are considerable in a number of Asian countries to develop sound and comprehensive international digital payments frameworks. Remittances are undoubtedly very important to economies in Asia, and the COVID-19 pandemic has boosted the positive role that remittances play. With focused policies and political willingness from governments and regulators, and a proactive private sector, a successful digital payments environment can be achieved.

Innovation and partnerships are beginning to take place, as demonstrated in the case studies of the Philippines, Malaysia, and Pakistan. These need to be built upon and expanded across the region. Comprehensive road maps for increasing digital payments, and pilot studies, can be developed to aid remittance recovery and growth in Asia from the COVID-19 pandemic.

# References

Alliance for Financial Inclusion (AFI). 2018. *Innovative cross-border remittance services: experiences from AFI member countries.* https://www.afi-global.org/sites/default/files/publications/2018-09/AFI_DFS_cross%20border_AW_digital.pdf.

Asian Development Bank (ADB). 2016. *Digital Payment Systems, Mobile Money Services, and Agent Banking: Bangladesh, Nepal, and Sri Lanka.* Manila. https://www.adb.org/sites/default/files/project-document/195971/48190-001-tacr.pdf.

———. 2017. Implementation Completion Memorandum, Bangladesh: Institutional Support for Migrant Workers' Remittances, Project Number 42149-012.

———. 2018a. *Asian Economic Integration Report 2018: Toward Optimal Provision of Regional Public Goods in Asia and the Pacific.* Manila: ADB. https://www.adb.org/sites/default/files/publication/456491/aeir-2018.pdf.

———. 2018b. *Migration and Remittances for Development in Asia.* Manila: ADB. https://www.adb.org/sites/default/files/publication/419611/migration-remittances-development-asia.pdf.

———. 2020. *COVID-19 Impact on International Migration, Remittances, and Recipient Households in Developing Asia.* Manila.

Bangladesh Bank. 2020. 4 December. https://www.bb.org.bd/en/index.php/mediaroom/circular.

Bank for International Settlements. 2018. Innovative technology in financial supervision (suptech) – the experience of early users. https://www.bis.org/fsi/publ/insights9.pdf.

*The Daily Star.* 2021, February 20. *Rise in Remittance in 2020: Bangladesh One of Three Large Recipients.* https://www.thedailystar.net/backpage/news/remittance-2020-bangladesh-third-largest-recipient-2047861.

Economynext. 2020. *Sri Lanka Remittances Down 23-pct in May but Up from April.* 30 June. https://economynext.com/sri-lanka-remittances-down-23-pct-in-may-but-up-from-april-71558/.

*Fiji Village.* 2021. Record Remittances in 2020 as $652.75 Million Was Sent through to Families in Fiji by Fijians Abroad. 3 March. https://www.fijivillage.com/feature/Record-remittances-in-2020-as-65275-million-was-sent-through-to-families-in-Fiji-by-Fijians-abroad-5frx48/.

*The Financial Express.* 2020, May 4. *Remittance Drops 25pc in April.* https://thefinancialexpress.com.bd/economy/bangladesh/remittance-drops-25pc-in-april-1588563129.

*Focus Economics.* 2020. *Philippines Remittances April 2020.* 4 January. https://www.focus-economics.com/countries/philippines/news/remittances/cash-remittances-record-largest-fall-on-record-in-april.

*Foreign Policy.* 2021. *The Pandemic May Change Remittances—for the Better.* 8 February. https://foreignpolicy.com/2021/02/08/the-pandemic-may-change-remittances-for-the-better/.

Global Knowledge Partnership on Migration and Development (KNOMAD). 2020. *COVID-19 Remittances Call to Action.* https://www.knomad.org/covid-19-remittances-call-to-action/.

Global System for Mobile Communications Association (GSMA). 2016. *The impact of mobile money interoperability in Tanzania.* https://www.gsma.com/mobilefordevelopment/wp-content/uploads/2016/10/2016_GSMA_The-impact-of-mobile-money-interoperability-in-Tanzania.pdf.

———. 2019. *State of the Industry Report on Mobile Money.* https://www.gsma.com/sotir/wp-content/uploads/2020/03/GSMA-State-of-the-Industry-Report-on-Mobile-Money-2019-Full-Report.pdf.

———. 2020a. *How Mobile Money Is Scaling International Remittances and Fostering Financial Resilience: Learnings from Valyou in Malaysia.* https://www.gsma.com/mobilefordevelopment/wp-content/uploads/2021/01/GSMA_How-mobile-money-is-scaling-international-remittances-1.pdf.

———. 2020b. *State of the Industry Report on Mobile Money.* London.

International Finance Corporation (IFC). 2016. *Mitigating the effects of de-risking in emerging markets to preserve remittance flows.* https://www.ifc.org/wps/wcm/connect/45fa0bf6-2ed2-4c57-9ada-298d1eb96c53/Note+22+EMCompass+-+De-Risking+and+Remittances++FINAL.pdf?MOD=AJPERES&CVID=lwwldO4.

International Fund for Agricultural Development (IFAD). 2015. *The Use of Remittances and Financial Inclusion.* Rome: IFAD.

IFAD. 2021. International Day of Family Remittances.

International Monetary Fund (IMF). 2020. *Samoa.* https://www.adb.org/sites/default/files/linked-documents/50028-003-imf-sam.pdf.

International Organization for Migration (IOM). 2020. *Rapid Assessment of the Socioeconomic Impacts of COVID-19 on Labour Mobility in the Pacific Region.* Geneva. https://publications.iom.int/system/files/pdf/iom-rapid-assessment-report.pdf.

PayPal. 2017. *Digital Payments: Thinking Beyond Transactions.* https://www.paypalobjects.com/digitalassets/c/website/marketing/global/shared/global/media-resources/documents/PayPal_Asia_Research_Report_Digital_Payments.pdf.

*PYMNTS.COM.* 2021. Malaysia's Mobile Money, Bangladesh's bKash Team With Ripple On eWallet Remittances. https://www.pymnts.com/news/blockchain-distributed-ledger/2021/malaysias-mobile-money-bangladeshs-bkash-team-with-ripple-on-ewallet-remittances/.

Rahman, M.M. and B.S.A. Yeoh. 2014. Social Organization of *Hundi*: Informal Remittance Transfer to South Asia. In Rahman M.M., Yong T.T., Ullah A.K.M.A. eds. Migrant Remittances in South Asia. International Political Economy Series. London: Palgrave Macmillan.

Ratha, D. 2020. *Remittances: Funds for the Folks Back Home.* https://www.imf.org/external/pubs/ft/fandd/basics/remitt.htm.

Reserve Bank of Australia (RBA). 2020. South Pacific Central Bank Governors Committed to Cost Effective Remittances. Joint media release. 20 November. https://www.rba.gov.au/media-releases/2020/mr-20-31.html.

Review42. 2020. *39+ Smartphone Statistics You Should Know in 2020.* https://review42.com/resources/smartphone-statistics//.

Sholevar, M., and Harris, L. 2020. 'Women are invisible?! A literature survey on gender gap and financial training,' *Citizenship, Social and Economic Education.* 19(2). pp. 87–99.

State Bank of Pakistan. 2019. *National Payment Systems Strategy: Road to Digital Payments.* https://www.sbp.org.pk/PS/PDF/NPSS.pdf.

———. 2020. *Measures to Limit the Spread of COVID-19 by Promoting the Use of Digital Payment Services.*

———. 2021. *Country-wise workers remittances.* https://www.sbp.org.pk/Ecodata/Homeremit.pdf.

United Nations. 2019a. *Global Compact for Safe, Orderly and Regular Migration. 73/195.* https://www.un.org/en/ga/search/view_doc.asp?symbol=A/RES/73/195.

———. 2019b. Remittances Matter: 8 Facts You Don't Know About The Money Migrants Send Back Home. News. 17 June.

United Nations, Department of Economic and Social Affairs (UNDESA). 2019. *International Migrant Stock by Destination and Origin.* https://www.un.org/en/development/desa/population/migration/data/estimates2/estimates19.asp.

———. 2020. Total Population.

World Bank. 2017. *Global Financial Inclusion (Global Findex) Database 2017.* https://microdata.worldbank.org/index.php/catalog/3324.

———. 2018. *Bilateral Remittance Matrix.* http://pubdocs.worldbank.org/en/705611533661084197/bilateralremittancematrix2017-Apr2018.xlsx.

———. 2020a. *COVID-19: Remittance Flows to Shrink 14% by 2021.* https://www.worldbank.org/en/news/press-release/2020/10/29/covid-19-remittance-flows-to-shrink-14-by-2021.

———. 2020b. *COVID-19 Crisis through a Migration Lens.* Migration and Development Brief 32.Washington, DC: World Bank.

———. 2020c. Migration and Development Brief 33. Washington, DC.

———. 2020d. *Pacific Island Countries in the Era Of Covid-19: Macroeconomic Impacts and Job Prospects.*http://documents1.worldbank.org/curated/en/835131608739709618/pdf/Pacific-Island-Countries-inthe-Era-of-COVID-19-Macroeconomic-Impacts-and-Job-Prospects.pdf.

———. 2020e. *Remittance Prices Worldwide.* https://remittanceprices.worldbank.org/en/data-download.

World Economic Forum (WEF). 2020. 4 Critical Steps for Fighting a Historic Remittance Decline in South Asia. 7 August. https://www.weforum.org/agenda/2020/08/4-critical-steps-for-fighting-a-historic-remittance-decline-in-south-asia/.